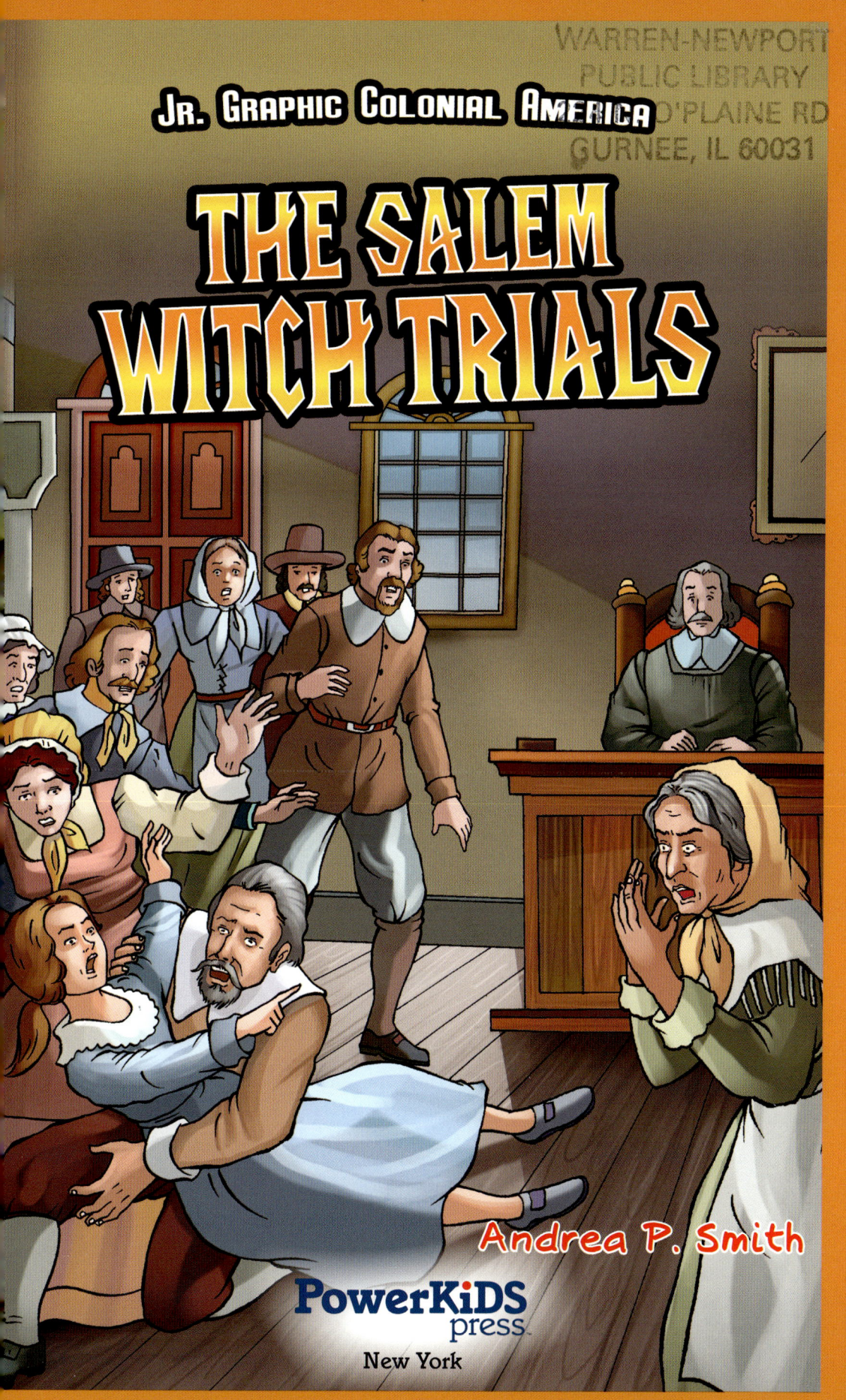

Published in 2012 by The Rosen Publishing Group, Inc.
29 East 21st Street, New York, NY 10010

Copyright © 2012 by The Rosen Publishing Group, Inc.

All rights reserved. No part of this book may be reproduced in any form without permission in writing from the publisher, except by a reviewer.

First Edition

Editor: Joanne Randolph
Book Design: Planman Technologies
Illustrations: Planman Technologies

Library of Congress Cataloging-in-Publication Data

Smith, Andrea P.
　The Salem witch trials / By Andrea P. Smith. — 1st ed.
　　p. cm. — (Jr. Graphic Colonial America)
Includes index.
ISBN 978-1-4488-5188-1 (library binding) — ISBN 978-1-4488-5214-7 (pbk.) — ISBN 978-1-4488-5215-4 (6-pack)
1. Trials (Witchcraft)—Massachusetts—Salem—Juvenile literature.
2. Witchcraft—Massachusetts—Salem—History—Juvenile literature. I. Title.
KFM2478.8.W5S65 2012
364.1'88—dc22

2010053124

Manufactured in the United States of America

CPSIA Compliance Information: Batch #PLS1102PK: For Further Information contact Rosen Publishing, New York, New York at 1-800-237-9932

Contents

Main Characters	3
The Salem Witch Trials	4
Timeline	22
Glossary	23
Index and Web Sites	24

Main Characters

Samuel Parris (1653–1720) Minister in Salem Village, Massachusetts. His daughter, Elizabeth (Betty), and niece, Abigail Williams, were the first girls to **accuse** people of being witches.

Rebecca Nurse (?–1692) Respected member of the Salem Village community who was accused of being a witch. Even though many people **testified** for her, she was found guilty of being a witch.

John Proctor (?–1692) A rich tavern keeper. He was accused of being a witch and found guilty.

Governor Sir William Phips (1651–1695) Governor of Massachusetts. He formed a special **court** for the witch **trials** and later let all the prisoners go.

William Stoughton (1631–1701) Judge at the witchcraft trials. He did not follow courtroom **procedures** and made it easier for **innocent** people to be found guilty of witchcraft.

THANK YOU FOR COMING, DOCTOR. WE'RE VERY WORRIED.
WHERE ARE THE GIRLS?
THEY'RE THIS WAY.
WHY ARE THEY BARKING LIKE DOGS?
WE DON'T KNOW.
PLEASE HELP THEM.
THEY MUST BE UNDER A WITCH'S SPELL.
OH NO!

TELL US WHO DID THIS TO YOU.
IT WAS TITUBA! SHE'S A WITCH.
NO!

SARAH GOOD IS A WITCH, TOO, AND SO IS SARAH OSBORNE.
THEY WILL HAVE TO PAY FOR THIS.

WHEN GOVERNOR PHIPS HEARD ABOUT THE WITCH TRIALS, HE FORMED A SPECIAL COURT.

WILLIAM, I WANT YOU TO BE THE JUDGE FOR THESE TRIALS. I TRUST YOU TO BE FAIR.

I'LL DO MY BEST, GOVERNOR.

I AM THE NEW JUDGE HERE, AND I WILL RID SALEM OF ALL WITCHES.

TIMELINE

1638 — Salem Village is settled by a small group of Puritans.

1672 — Salem Village is allowed to begin a new parish and hire a minister.

1689 — Salem Village Church is formed, and Samuel Parris is brought in as the minister.

January 1692 — Girls in Salem Village start having fits. The doctor decides that a witch is to blame for their fits. The girls start accusing people of being witches.

February 1692 — Doctor Griggs examines the girls and believes witchcraft is to blame for their behavior.

February 1692 — Magistrates John Hathorne and Jonathan Corwin look for witches' marks on the accused.

March 1692 — Rebecca Nurse is accused of being a witch.

May 1692 — Governor Phips sets up a special court for the witch trials.

June 1692 — Bridget Bishop is the first person to be hanged for witchcraft.

July 1692 — Rebecca Nurse and four other women are hanged for witchcraft.

August 1692 — John Proctor was hanged.

October 29, 1692 — Governor Phips puts a stop to the special court.

May 1693 — Governor Phips clears all prisoners of the crime of witchcraft.

1752 — Salem Village changes its name to Danvers.

May 9, 1992 — The Salem Witch Trials Memorial was opened to the public on the 300th anniversary of the Salem Witch Trials.

Glossary

accuse (uh-KYOOZ) To say someone did something bad.

Barbados (bahr-BAY-dus) An island country in the West Indies.

convicted (kun-VIKT-ed) Found or proved someone guilty.

court (KORT) The place where people who break rules or laws are judged.

evidence (EH-vuh-dunts) Facts that prove something.

examined (ig-ZA-mund) Looked closely at.

hysteria (his-TER-ee-uh) Strong feelings or great fear.

innocence (IH-nuh-sens) Having done nothing wrong.

memorial (meh-MOR-ee-ul) Something used as a reminder of a person, a place, or an event.

procedures (pruh-SEE-jurz) Steps or rules to follow.

spirit (SPIR-it) The soul of a dead person.

testified (TES-tih-fyd) Spoke in court about the facts of a trial.

testimony (TES-tuh-moh-nee) Statements made by people under oath.

trials (TRY-ulz) When cases are decided in court.

INDEX

A
accuse(d), 3, 4, 5, 12, 14, 18, 20

B
Barbados, 7

C
convicted, 14
court, 3, 11, 15, 16
courtroom procedures, 3

E
evidence, 13

F
fits, 8, 14

G
Good, Sarah, 10, 21
guilty, 3, 13, 17

H
hanged, 13, 15, 19, 21
hysteria, 5

I
illegal, 17
innocence, 5
innocent, 3, 12, 18, 19

J
jail, 21
judge, 3, 16

L
law, 17

M
marks, 5, 11, 12
minister, 3, 6

N
Nurse, Rebecca, 3, 4, 12, 13, 14, 21

O
Osborne, Sarah, 10

P
Parris, Elizabeth (Betty), 3
Parris, Samuel, 3, 6, 8
Phips, Sir William, 3, 16, 19
prisoner(s), 3, 19
Proctor, Elizabeth, 14
Proctor, John, 3, 14

S
Salem Witch Trials Memorial, 20
Salem Village, Massachusetts, 3, 4, 6, 16, 18
spirit, 8, 17, 18
Stoughton, William, 3, 17

T
testified, 3, 15
testimony, 17
Tituba, 6, 8, 10
trial(s), 3, 16, 18, 21

W
Williams, Abigail, 3
witchcraft, 3
witch's mark(s), 5, 12
witch's spell, 9
witch trials, 3, 4, 16, 19, 21

WEB SITES

Due to the changing nature of Internet links, Power Kids Press has developed an online list of Web sites related to the subject of this book. This site is updated regularly. Please use this link to access the list:

www.powerkidslinks.com/JGCO/salem